D0516943

SPLIT
HISTORY · CULTURE · ART HERITAGE

Published by
FORUM - ZADAR
NAKLADA ŠOKOTA

Written, edited and designed by
ANTUN TRAVIRKA

Photographs by
ANDRIJA CARLI

Editor-in-Chief and Responsible Editor
ĐURĐICA ŠOKOTA

For the Publisher
ŽIVKO ŠOKOTA

Translated by
VJEKOSLAV SUZANIĆ

Set and printed by
GORENJSKI TISK, KRANJ, SLOVENIA 2000

© FORUM - ZADAR, 2000

All rights reserved. No part of this book may be duplicated,
photocopied, or reproduced in any way without
a prior written permission of the Publisher.

CIP - Katalogizacija u publikaciji
Znanstvena knjižnica u Zadru
UDK 914.975(036) SPLIT
    338.48:659.2 SPLIT

TRAVIRKA, Antun
    Split : History, culture, art heritage / [written, edited
and designed by] Antun Travirka ; [photographs by
Andrija Carli ; translated by Vjekoslav Suzanić].
- Zadar : Forum ; Naklada Šokota, 2000. - 80 str. : ilustr. ;
24 cm + [1] folded sheet with city plan

Izv. stv. nasl. : Split : povijest, kultura, umjetnička baština

ISBN 953-179-376-X

SPLIT

HISTORY · CULTURE · ART HERITAGE

ANTUN TRAVIRKA

FORUM

Two millenia of Split

Split is the largest city on the Croatian coast of the Adriatic Sea; after Zagreb it is the second largest in Croatia. It is an important economic, traffic, cultural, religious, research, educational, sports and tourist centre. It is the administrative seat of the County of Split-Dalmatia. The wider region of Split comprises the city of Split and the cities of Solin and Kaštela, while continuous urban area stretches from the town of Trogir in the west to the town of Omiš in the east, at mouth of the river Cetina. This long but narrow urban agglomeration, with Split at its centre, is almost 60 km long but only 5 km wide. It comprises the Gulf of Kaštela, the lower flow of the river Jadro, the peninsula on which Split is situated, and the coast as far as the mouth of the river Cetina. The continental hinterland is enclosed with the high Dinaric mountain ranges of Kozjak and Mosor. A deep gorge is cut between these mountains at Klis, linking the seaboard with the continental hinterland. We can also include in wider region of Split the eastern part of the island of Čiovo and the

island of Šolta. Owing to the protection of the high mountains, the area is protected from the influence of the continental climate, and the climate is exceptionally mild and favourable for the development of typical Mediterranean vegetation. Morphologically varied, exceptionally functional and expressly attractive area with high mountains in the background, a deep pass providing possibility of communication with the continent, with a spacious and deep bay protected by the islands, and long massive points, an abundance of healthy water at the base of the mountains and with a fertile soil surrounding the bay - it has been attractive to man for habitation ever since early prehistory.

The earliest finds of the presence of man in the area are stone artefacts from the Middle Palaeolithic age (about 50,000 years BC) which were found in the Mujo cave above the field of Kaštela. In the New Stone Age people still lived in caves, but probably also in settlements in the islets in the delta of the Jadro. In the Eneolithic period the first hill-fort settlements appear. Finds of gold artefacts on the Gripe Heights are proof of such a fort in the Split peninsula. In the Bronze and Iron Ages this area was populated by the Illyrian tribe of the Delmatae, from whom the name of the whole region derived. A whole series of Illyrian hill-forts are found on the heights of Kozjak while their larger settlements developed in the coastal area. The Greeks founded their first colonies in the area in the 4th century BC. Besides the existing Illyrian settlements they founded their cities of Tragurion (Trogir), Salonae (Solin) and Epetion (Stobreč). The city of Salonae was situated at an exceptionally convenient place, at the mouth of the Jadro and at the crossing of the road running along the Adriatic coast and the road leading to the interior over the pass of Klis. In the period of Roman domination Salonae developed into a large city which became the administrative, economic and religious centre of the whole of the east coast of the Adriatic. In the time of Emperor August in the 1st century BC, Salonae was given the status of a colony (Colonia Martia Iulia Salonae). Until its conquest and destruction by the Avars and the Slavs the city of Salonae had been growing continuously, and big complexes of profane and cultic architecture were built there. The fragments of ruins even nowadays reveal that it was a great, systematically built, and an important cosmopolitan Mediterranean city. According to some estimates, when it was at highest the city probably had as many as 60,000 inhabitants. The ruins of Salonae are among are among the most important archaeological sites on the east coast of the Adriatic Sea. Complexes of church buildings and a number of large Christian graveyards at Salonae and its surroundings are of especial importance for the study of early Christianity. Archaeological investigations at Salonae have been conducted for almost two centuries, and generations of Croatian and foreign archaeologists have contributed to the reconstruction of the area, the disposition of the urban web and of

Archaeological Museum, Early Christian sarcophagus with the figure of the Good Shepherd

the complex forms of urban life in classical antiquity. Especial notice should be given to Frane Bulić, whose exceptional contribution was in the study of the period of early Christianity in the area of Salonae. It was owing to his merits that the First International Congress of Early Christian Archaeology was held at Solin in 1894. The same significance for his contribution to the understanding of life in Salonae in classical antiquity is due to the famous Danish archaeologist Einar Dyggve, who investigated this area in the nineteen-twenties.

In close vicinity, on a little tongue of land, in a cove then named Aspalathos was situated a Greek settlement of the same name, probably very small. (Aspalathos is the Greek name for the Mediterranean shrub Spanish broom, a plant which in early spring blooms with tiny, intensive yellow flowers). In the Roman period it was named Spalatum, as can be seen from the preserved copy of a Roman road map which had been drawn before the palace of Diocletian was built. The location of the settlement has not yet been positively identified in the city core of present-day Split, but during archaeological investigations of the eastern part of the Palace of Diocletian architectural remains were found, which prove

Emperor Diocletian, portrait on a Roman coin

the existence of an urban structure, or at least of a larger representative temporal or cultic complex which had existed in the area before the construction of the palace. The most recent archaeological investigations conducted in the last years in the wider area of the city core present new data corroborating these assertions. The palace of the Roman emperor Diocletian was built at that very favourable site, at the bottom of the southern cove of the peninsula of Split, in the period between about 293 and 305. AD.

Gaius Aurelius Valerius Diocletianus was an Illyrian, born most probably at Salonae. The legions proclaimed him emperor in 284. His reign is remembered for great reforms in administration, especially for the division of the Empire in two parts and the introduction of the system of tetrarchy (two emperors and two caesars), because of its size and the difficulties of administration of the huge area from one centre. In 293 he chose for his area the eastern part of the Empire with the administrative centre at Nicomedia, a city in Bithynia on the coast of the Sea of Marmara (today in Tur-

key). By then he had probably started his palace, his retreat after abdication. The builders had doubtless come from the east: two inscribed Greek names, Zotikos and Phylatos, testify to that. The stone materials for the palace were brought partly from the quarries on the island of Brač, but also from the surroundings of Trogir. The Architectural ornaments and the marble slabs used for the facings were imported from the Italian peninsula, from the Greek islands, and especially from Egypt. After his abdication in 305, Diocletian moved to a very spacious fortified palace of quadrangular plan, defended by strong walls and powerful towers. A mausoleum was built in the palace itself, to receive the emperor's body after his death. After his death in 316. the palace remained in the possession of the Roman emperors. It is a known fact that the last but one emperor of the Western empire Julius Nepos took refuge in the palace in 475. At the close of the 4th century a weaving mill was mentioned in the palace.

In the 7th century the Avars and the Slavs penetrated in the area of the Gulf of Kaštela and utterly destroyed the city

Peristyle with prothyrum

of Salonae, so that it never recovered. The surviving population fled to the neighbouring islands, and a considerable part, led by certain Severus, took refuge within the walls of the Palace. In this way, the former country palace of the Roman emperor was soon transformed into the medieval city of Split. The imperial suites, the space in the corner towers and other fortifications, as well as all living quarters, were divided into smaller units and thus created the basis of the future urban fabric. The reorganisation of the Church of Salonae in 8th century gave special legitimacy to the new city, and so Split had its first archbishop, John of Ravenna. Diocletian's mausoleum was converted into a cathedral dedicated to the Virgin, but from 9th century it was frequently referred to as the church of St. Domnius, the first bishop of Salonae and Christian martyr who suffered during the severe persecution under Diocletian. Of the early medieval city chiefs there is a record of the name of prior Peter from 9th century, whose sarcophagus was preserved in the outer corridor of the cathedral. The palace gradually transformed into a medieval city not only by adaptation and alteration but also with the erection of new buildings within its area and with the growth of a larger western outskirts and a series of smaller sacral building on the periphery. The only square within the palace was the ancient Peristyle which served for both civic and religious functions.

In the Early Middle Ages Split was most of the time under Byzantine rule. But in its closest vicinity there grew in 9th century a new state under Croatian princes which was to grow strong in the 10th century. The Croatian king Tomislav was present at the important church councils in Split in 925 and 928. In 11th century Split was part of the Croatian state under King Peter Krešimir IV. King Stephen II, one of the last Croatian kings, retreated to the monastery of St. Stephen in Split.

From 1108, when King Collomanus confirmed its privileges, during the reign of Croato-Hungarian kings, Split enjoyed the status of a free community, which led to considerable prosperity, spreading and

Aqueduct from antiquity which supplied the Palace with water. In use even today.

growth. The city minted its own coins, and from 1312 it has had its own statute, compiled by the mayor Perceval of Fermo. From 1207 the citizens elected the priors or city rectors from among the distinguished Croatian and Bosnian feudal lords (Gregory of Bribir, Paul and Mladen Šubić, Hrvoje Vukčić). The life in the medieval city commune was rather stormy. Documents record frequent wars and fights with the population living along the shores of the Cetina river, Omiš, Trogir, the danger of the Mongol conquest in 1242, the conflicts between the commune and the Archdiocese, and the uprising of the populace against the feudal masters in 1398. The monumental belfry of the cathedral was built during this period, and the former western suburb became an integral part of the city when it was enclosed with a defending wall. This new part of the city took over the role of the municipal centre, and a new town hall was built in St. Lawrence Square. Outside the new city walls in the western side a new suburb developed around the church of the Holy Cross. Two important monasteries

Sarcophagus of prior Peter (8-9th c.) on the outer perimeter of the cathedral

Sarcophagus of archbishop John of Ravenna (Ivan Ravenjanin) (7-8th c.), cathedral baptistery

were built in this period outside the wall - the Franciscan and the Dominican.

For a short time in the 14th century, from 1327 to 1357, Split was under Venetian domination. During dynastic fighting for the Hungarian-Croatian crown, King Ladislas of Naples ceded in 1409 his royal right over Dalmatia to Venice for 100,000 ducats. This was the start of the process of definite subjugation of Dalmatian city communes to the Venetian authority. Split fell under the authority of the Venetian Republic in 1420, and it would remain so until the fall of the republic and its abolition in 1797. For its garrison in Split Venice built a citadel with two impressive large towers at the south-west corner of the palace of Diocletian in 1435. A teacher of the communal school first appears in a document from 1434. In 15th and early 16th century a number of palaces were built or reconstructed in flowering Gothic style, and later in Gothic-Renaissance style. Most notable in this respect is a complex of city palaces in St. Lawrence Square, built in flowering Gothic style but largely pulled down, unfortunately, in the first half of 19th century. The most distinguished Dalmatian builder and sculptor Juraj Matejev Dalmatinac executed many of his building and sculptural projects in those times. The sculptor Bonino of Milan and the painter Dujam Vušković of Split distinguished themselves side by side with him. At the same time, Marko Marulić, great Renaissance poet and Father of Croatian literature was active in Split. Together with numerous works in Latin, he completed in 1501 the first full work in the Croatian literary language, the epic "Judita" (Judith). An important circle of humanists of various profiles was also active with him.

The first penetrations of the Turks to Split area were recorded around 1500. For almost two centuries Split and its

Left:
The central area of the Palace of Diocletian with the Peristyle, the mausoleum (today cathedral) and Romanesque belfry

environs, as well as other parts of the Croatian seaboard, would live in immediate danger of conquest. Yet in the periods of peace trade connections with the hinterland would develop.

The idea of Daniel Rodriga, a Split merchant became gradually reality in the last quarter of 16th century. Split was to become the principal Venetian port for the trade with the Balkans. For this purpose, large warehouses with facilities for disinfection of goods, lodgings for merchants and cattle drivers, stables, custom house and lazarettos were completed in 1592 close to the south-eastern corner of Diocletian's Palace. Armed escorts were provided for sea transport of goods from Venice to Split. In this way Split became an important stage on the commercial road from Sarajevo, Skoplje, and Sophia to Constantinople, and goods and merchants arrived even from Persia and India. The first bank was established in Split as early as 1592 because of great credit activity. Great circulation of people coming from the East caused several severe epidemics of plague which decimated the population of Split in 17th century. In that period, during the Candian War and immediate threat of the Turks, the Venetian administration built a strong system of fortification with pentagonal bastions encircling the whole city, and independent forts were built on the Gripe Height and the south-eastern point of the port of Split. In 17th and 18 centuries Split had its notable intellectual circle. Among others, its members were the archbishop and scholar Markantun Dominis, the poet Jerolim Kavanjin and the composer Julije Bajamonti. The "Illyrian Academy" was founded in 1704 with the aim of cultivation and use of the Croatian language. "Economic Academy" was founded as early as 1767, with the aim of propagating of progressive forms of agriculture, crafts and commerce.

Records from 1750 show that the nobles of Split produced an opera in the city theatre, which was situated in the Town Hall. In 1770, in the same theatre was produced the

13

oratorio "The Transfer of the relics of St. Domnius" by the composer and polyhistor Julije Bajamonti. The famous British architect Robert Adam, one of the first propagators of the classicist style in architecture, visited Split in 1757. He studied systematically the Palace of Diocletian and in 1674 published a representative work about it, which had decisive influence both for the development of archaeology in Europe and for the appearance and development of the classicist style in European art. The City hospital was built in Split in 1794.

After the fall of the Republic of Venice in 1797, Split was for a short time under Austrian authority, and from 1806 to 1813 under Napoleon. The short period of French administration is significant because of great building activities connected with the transformation of the city, partial destruction of the city walls, building of the embankment and of the park. Especial merit deserves the French marshal Marmont, military governor of Dalmatia at the time.

From 1813 until 1918 Split and the whole Dalmatia was under Austrian authority. During the major part of the 19th century Split was ruled by the "autonomous" city administration which vehemently opposed any idea of unifying Dalmatia and Croatia. The situation lasted until the decisive victory of the national Party at the city elections in 1882, since when Split and its nationally awakened new middle class led in the struggle for the unification of the littoral and the continental Croatia. Systematic building end extension of the city and regulation of the historic core continued during this whole period. The port was enlarged and protective break-water was built in the last quarter of the 19th century. The gas works were built in this period, the system of railways linking the mining sites in the hinterland was started in 1874, and then the line to the junction at Knin was started, to be completed in 1888. As Austrian authorities had no interest in linking Dalmatia with the continental part of

Left:
A view of the decumanus, principal transverse street in Diocletian's Palace

Aerial view of Narodni trg

Croatian, the first railway from Split to Zagreb via Lika was completed only after World War I, in 1925. Split was thus linked with the continental European centres for the first time. A series of important cultural and educational institutions was established in this period: the Archaeological museum, founded as early as 1821, Classical Grammar School in 1817, the Theatre in 1859, the new Municipal Theatre in 1893, and numerous schools and reading rooms, and organised sport activities were also recorded. As early as the middle of the century the architect and conservationist Vicko Andrić recorded the details of Diocletian's palace and prepared extensive plans for cleaning and restoration.

A strong intellectual and artistic circle with markedly national orientation formed in Split at the close of the century, which at the turn of the century played important role in the nascent stage of Croatian Modernism.

The football club "Hajduk", founded in 1911, has not only been the centre

Panorama of Split. Bačvice cove in the foreground, passenger harbour in the centre,
old city core on the right. Marjan peninsula in the background.

of sporting life and patriotic gathering in Split but it is also one of the oldest and most successful sport clubs in Croatia.

After the fall of the Austro-Hungarian Monarchy, Split became part of the Kingdom of the Serbs, Croats, and Slovenes, later the Kingdom of Yugoslavia. In that period it was the administrative centre of Dalmatia and the largest port in the country. A strong cement industry developed in the vicinity.

The city grew quickly and developed in the areas of earlier suburbs. The population more than doubled between the two world wars. In this period, too, Split was an distinctive, notable, significant, important, major, leading cultural centre. The sculptor Ivan Meštrović worked there occasionally, and the painter Emanuel Vidović madehis most mature works. Of especial importance is the development and work

of the theatre, and in this connection the work of noted Croatian composers Ivo Tijardović and Jakov Gotovac.

In World War II the city suffered from bombing, and it was occupied by the Kingdom of Italy until its capitulation in the autumn of 1943. After a year's new occupation by the Germans, Split was finally liberated in October 1944, since when it has been in the Republic of Croatia within the federal Yugoslavia. In the post-war period Split developed very dynamically, and the population multiplied several times. An important industrial complex developed, with the production of cement, shipbuilding, chemical, metal-working and food processing industry. As for transport, Split extended and specialised its port capacities; roads, railways, and a modern airport at Kaštela were built. Tourist activities started in the period between the wars, while modern development transformed Split into an important tourist centre of the whole area of central Adriatic. Numerous cultural monuments and its two millennia of history attract tourists from all over the world, as do the natural beauties of its surroundings. University departments were established at Split In the early sixties, particularly such as were necessary for the education of personnel in the growing industrial production, economy, administration, education and traffic. The university was incorporated in 1974. Nowadays it has 18 faculties and colleges. Split is also the seat of several scholarly institutes. New museums were built, theatre activities were extended, important sport facilities were built, some of them among the most beautiful in Croatia. Split is also an important Croatian centre of newspaper and book publishing.

In conformity with the international convention of world cultural and natural heritage, UNESCO accepted in 1974 the proposal that the historic core of Split with the palace of Diocletian be inscribed in the list of world heritage. As the best preserved example of an imperial palace from classical antiquity, it is considered all over the world as the key building for the understanding of that type of architecture; and the palace has exerted exceptional influence on urban development and architecture in European relations.

In the War of Croatian Independence, 1991-1995, the defence of Split was exceptionally decisive and effective, and masses of the fighters from Split took part in the war operations on many Croatian battlefields. Today Split is the centre of a county, administrative, economic and financial centre of Dalmatia, but also a centre to which the western part of the neighbouring state of Bosnia and Herzegovina gravitates.

The Palace of Emperor Diocletian

The architectural and cultural-historical monuments of Split are for the greater part concentrated in the area of the historical city core, so it is most logical to start the tour of the sights from the very centre of the old core - the palace of Diocletian. It is generally considered that the emperor had the palace built in order to retire to it at the time of his prearranged abdication in favour of the caesar who was his deputy. Historical facts prove this for the most part, because he had spent the last years of his life in the palace - from the abdication at Nicomedia on May 1, 305 until his death around

Reconstruction of the original view of the palace of Diocletian after E. Hèbrard

Egyptian sphinx in the Peristyle

monarchy appeared the new cult of the emperor as deity, Jupiter's son, which was promulgated while the emperor was still alive. Four tetrarchs were thus to symbolise four seasons, four basic elements and were living deities walking the earth. The core of the Split palace with the Peristyle and four temples is analysed in this light, and it is obvious that it was not built just as an imperial mausoleum but also as the centre of the new cult of the divine emperor - while he was still alive. Another fact should be added to this: that the form of government in his time - considering unquiet borders and the size of the empire- demanded that the court often move, which is proved by several imperial residences of Diocletian (like the ones at Sirmium, Nicomedia, Palmyra and Antioch), but also the residences of the other tetrarchs. All this leads to the conclusion that the palace was built as the imperial court, the capital of the ruling emperor, particularly if the geographic and strategic position of Salonae, almost in the centre of the empire is taken into consideration. It was only a severe illness that forced Diocletian to abdicate in 305, forced him to retire to the palace which had not yet been completed in all details.

The complex of the Palace of Diocletian has the form of a slightly deformed quadrilateral. The longer sides are 215 m long, and the narrower ones, north and south, are about 180 m long. The total area of the complex of the palace is about 30,000 sq. metres. It was built according to the taste and ideas of the eastern part of the Roman empire, and at the same time it represented a highly sumptuous imperial villa, Hellenistic town and strongly fortified military camp.

A transverse street from the western to the eastern gate cuts the palace complex in two. The southern half was intended for the imperial suites and cult, and the northern half consisted of two large residential blocks for the servants and the protective garrison. Strong outer defensive wall was reinforced at the corners with four massive quadrangular towers, and each wall face, except for the one towards the sea, with two additional smaller towers of quadrangular plan. Each of the land gates was flanked with two octagonal towers. The Palace was thus defended by 16 forts. The land walls of the palace were in their upper part opened with large windows with simple arches, and the south wall, facing the sea, was articulated with garlands, consoles and half-pillars. Along the walls ran a guard passage. As the medieval city grew into the palace with the passage of time, a significant part of the

the year 316. A new analysis of the available historical sources as well as studies of the purposefulness of the construction of the palace (J. Belamarić, 1999) seem to cast a new light on these monumental remains. It is undeniable fact that Diocletian had a very successful military campaign against the rebels in Egypt between 297 and 298. A total of 11 Egyptian sphinxes were found in the area of the palace, and all the columns in the palace are made of precious kinds of stone - red, rose and grey granite, porphyry, and white marble from Egyptian temples and other representative Egyptian buildings. This can be proved by the fact that the column capital are of unequal heights, because they were carved at the site in order to make all columns equal in height. Such a large shipment of precious architectural decoration from Egypt confirms that it was the emperor's personal dispatch, and indirectly, according to this interpretation, it puts the year 298 as the possible date when the building began. This new way of thinking points to a change in the religious understanding which occurred at the time of Diocletian and the rule of the tetrarchs, when in the application of the oriental form of absolute

Vertical aerial photograph of the historical core of Split. Palace of Diocletian to the right, former western outskirts integrated into the city walls during the Middle Ages to the left, People's Square in the centre.

The north face

the passage of time, a significant part of the original architecture was preserved, but mostly used for completely different function. Still, even in this state, the Palace is the best preserved complex of late Roman court architecture in the world. Reconstruction and conservation work has been going on for almost two centuries, and have been especially intensive for the last fifty years. This work is so complex that it will doubtless continue for many years to come. Nevertheless, all essential components of the Palace have been systematically analysed, and the conclusions concerning its construction, functioning and reconstruction during many centuries can be given with a high degree of certainty.

Approaching the palace from land we can conclude that the north wall is preserved for almost its whole length, and it is there that we can visualise the dimension of the palace. The octagonal and the quadrangular forts were pulled down, but their positions are clearly evident. The whole area along the north face was filled 1.5 metres, so the proportions of the city gate and other architectural details are somewhat distorted when compared to the original composition. The large arched window openings at the upper level of the front have been preserved and are visible, although filled in. The centre of the north face is decorated with a monumental gate, later to be named *Porta aurea - Golden Gate*. Of all the

Interior of early mediaeval church of St. Martin above the north gate of the palace of Diocletian

tel with the inscription of priest Dominic, the barrel vault of the church and three small windows with stone rails set in the original arched openings of the palace turned to the defensive yard but now filled in - are preserved to the present day in original positions. In the early Middle Ages a belfry was built above the church, probably of the same character as the one preserved at the Western gate of the Palace. Later it was pulled down and a low bell tower built in its place, which existed as late as the 18th century, as it can be seen in contemporary copper engravings. The *north-west corner tower* is also preserved very well. The ground-floor has cylindrical intersecting vaults. There are two largish window openings, and the third floor is covered with wooden construction of four eaves and admits light through three large windows on each side. In the early Middle Ages the tower was adapted into the church of St. Peter, and from 11th century it was within the complex of the Benedictine nunnery. It was therefore often referred to as Arnir's tower. Later the upper floor was pulled down in order to establish a passage for the guards. In 17th c. it was furnished with cannon. The tower was repaired recently, and it houses the Mediterranean Centre for Architectural Heritage of the University of Split and post-graduate studies of the same subject. The

Remains of the defence court of the East gate to the Palace of Diocletian

four entrances to the palace they are architecturally most pronounced, and was doubtless the main entrance at the point where the road from Salonae ended. Two niches on the side of the gate, and three niches above the entrance, as well as semicircular arches which were formerly supported by pillars are the principal decoration on the external side. The whole complex is enriched with ornamental stone capitals and consoles. The capital on the western side of the gate is inscribed with the Greek name ZOTIKOS, which is one of extremely rare, but important piece of information about the origin of the builder. Four column bases are preserved above the wall, originally probably carrying the statues of the emperor Diocletian and the other three tetrarchs, emperor Maximianus and two caesars-successors, Galerius and Constantius Chlorus. On the internal side, the gate has an impressive and monumental defensive yard, *propugnaculum*. It served as the last stand in case of enemy penetration through the gate. Part of the guard passage above the gate was converted in Early Middle Ages to a small *church of St. Martin*. The original pre-Romanesque altar rail with votive inscription to Blessed Martin and the Blessed Virgin Mary, the lin-

The eastern gate of the Palace of Diocletian ("Silver Gate")

The east wall of the palace

north-eastern tower was identical to the former, but it was adapted into residences in 18th century. The original wall from classical antiquity is preserved to the level of the first floor.

The eastern wall can be observed in its full length, but later modifications have disturbed the rhythm of the openings in the wall. The quadrangular and the octagonal towers were pulled down in the 17th century, a the present-day situation, particularly of the part from the gate to the south-eastern corner tower, was greatly affected by the addition of a castle of the duke Hrvoje Vukčić Hrvatinić in 15th century, and its subsequent removal. The additions have been recently removed, and the wall was reconstructed if and where sufficient elements were available. *The Eastern Gate,* later named *Silver Gate,* is similar to the northern gate, but considerably more modest in composition and decoration. It was reconstructed, and even closed several times in the course of centuries. In 18th century, after the end of the Turkish threat, a new, smaller gate was opened in the eastern wall at a position more to the north. The Silver gate was reopened and reconstructed in the late forties, while the interior defence court was partly renewed in 1952. *The South-western tower* originally had the ground floor and three floors above, i.e. was a floor higher that the two north ones because the ground on which the palace was built descends to the sea slowly. Of the same for was also the *South-western tower,* now pulled down. The south-eastern tower is now preserved to the second floor, with a flat terrace above it. The upper floors of the tower were part of the bishop's palace during the Middle Ages. The modification of the first floor with Gothic vault is from that period. The windows of the second floor are filled in, but are clearly recognisable from the outside.

The remains of the western wall

The western wall of the palace suffered most because the city spread towards the west. It was partly pulled down, and part of it grew into new building complexes. The south-western corner tower was demolished completely, while the remains of the western wall can best be seen at Mihovilova širina. The remains of the medieval *church of St. Michael "at the seashore"* from 7th or 8th century can be seen in the same area, the first church outside the walls of the Palace. (The church is linked with the activities of the first archbishop of Split, John of Ravenna.) At the time of building the church was indeed at the seashore, because a little cove was located close to the south-western tower at the site of the present-day Trg braće Radić. The original building had a single nave with a semi-circular apse, which can be seen from the remains of the

South-eastern corner tower of Diocletian's palace.

church. During subsequent enlargement a new apse was excavated in the western wall of the palace.

The *Western Gate,* called *Iron Gate*, was the principal link during the Middle Ages between the old city nucleus in the palace and the new suburb in the west. It does not differ in form from the Eastern Gate, but is in a much better state of preservation, especially its defence yard and parts of the octagonal towers on the outer side. The little *church of Our Lady of the Belfry* (originally church of St. Theodore) was built in the guard passage above the interior gate. Cylindrical intersecting vaults and belfry from 11th century are preserved from the original church, the oldest pre-Romanesque belfry on our side of the Adriatic. The belfry is articulated with characteristic openings at three floor levels. On the first and second floors it has small simple arched windows, and a double window on the third floor. Below the roof is a decorative belt suggesting blind arches, decoration characteristic of the oncoming Romanesque style.

Church of the Lady of the Belfry (St. Theodore) over the west gate to Diocletian's palace, 11th c.

Left:
Western gate of the Palace of Diocletian with well-preserved defence court

The southern face of the palace

The southern face of the palace differs essentially from the other three. Originally it was washed by the sea. A small, relatively insignificant gate, colloquially known as *"Brass Gate"* (Nos. 22-23, Obala narodnog preporoda) is in the centre, serving as immediate access to a galley. On the ground-floor there was a series of small openings, later filled in, but which are noticeable on the interior side of the wall in a long corridor. A long passage at the first floor level opened to the sea in a series of arched windows separated by half-columns. The rhythm of the windows was broken in the centre and at either end, and it was emphasized with raised tripartite openings (loggias). The passage had the function of a

long promenade with a direct view of the bay and the islands in the distance, but it was also the principal link between the various halls and the imperial apartments. Along the top of the wall ran a guard passage, which completely disappeared during subsequent modifications. The southern face of the palace was largely modified and hidden by later additions. It was only in the last decades that the less significant additions were gradually removed, which revealed the elements of the original form more clearly. After filling the embankment, picturesque little residential houses were built against the wall. During the purification of the palace area, in early 20th century, they were all pulled down, and were replaced in the period between the two world wars by buildings in the spirit of the traditional architecture of the German architect Keller. They have no historical or artistic value, but have given life to the area of the embankment.

The remains of the imperial suite

Diocletian's suite extended over the whole of the south quarter of the building to the height of two floors. The ground-floor (colloquially referred to as "Diocletian's cellars") was in fact a sub-structure, the constructive carrier of the suites on the first floor. It should be borne in mind that the ground under the palace falls obliquely towards the sea and that the ground structure partly served to level the total area of the Palace. The area of Diocletian's suite on the first floor was mainly destroyed with numerous modifications over the centuries, while the ground-floor sub-structure is in an excellent state of preservation and an excellent indication of the original plan of the imperial suites. The two basic axes of this area is the longitudinal axis consisting of the Vestibule and the central hall, and a transverse axis represented by the promenade along the southern face. All other suites were connected by this long passageway. Close to the central hall were smaller chambers of the emperor's personal guard. The western part consisted of reception halls and the personal suites of the emperor, while the eastern part consisted of the whole complex of the dining hall and other chambers the purpose of which has not been ascertained yet. At the first floor level, of the chambers comprising the longitudinal axis, it is only the *doorway to the central hall* in the south-

The door to the central hall of Diocletian's apartment

ern wall, its foundation walls, and the entrance hall - the *Vestibule* - that survive. The Vestibule is preserved in its bare state, but even so it can give an indication of the monumental character of the imperial suites. Access to the Vestibule is from the Peristyle. This is a hall which is quadrangular in form outside, but the interior is of a circular plan. It is articulated with half-round niches and vaulted with a cupola. The upper part of the vault of the cupola is destroyed. Its walls were originally lined with mosaics and decorative marble slabs. The sub-structure of the Vestibule on the ground-floor has the form of a cross. On the first floor, sections of the walls of the triclinium (dining hall) and minute sections of the walls of the western reception hall have been preserved. *Triclinium* is named after the dining-couch (triclinium) which the Romans used while dining in a half-reclining position leaning on an elbow. The dining hall of Diocletian's apartment extended over a large section of the eastern part of the palace. It consisted of a large central hall, three lesser halls and entrance halls. The large central hall is quadrangular on the outside, and the interior space is octagonal, additionally articulated with semi-circular niches. The lesser halls were in the shape of a cross. Some walls of the western hall of the triclinium are preserved almost up to the height of the roof, only the lower sections of the northern hall were discovered, while the eastern hall was destroyed completely.

The central hall of the triclinium was preserved in the lower sections of the wall only, but during recent conservation it was reconstructed to the height of about two metres. The convent of St. Claire was built in the area of the imperial dining hall in 14th century, but it was moved to a new position in 1883.

The eastern complex of the *baths - termae* was discovered to the north of the triclinium. The remains reveal a semi-circular pool for warm water - piscina - which was provided with a stove on one side, and a chamber with hot air - caldarium - on the other. A system of floor heating was discovered, consisting of a hollow space for the circulation of hot air and a large number of small clay posts supporting the floor. The vertical walls were heated through hollow bricks. An interesting find is a fragment of a water pipe made of lead.

The preserved fragments of the walls of *the western imperial reception hall*, as well as its sub-structure on the ground-floor which is completely preserved, show that this was a representative hall which as a central hall extended along the full width of Diocletian's apartment. While the sub-structure has load-bearing pylons, the hall on the first floor was probably a single area articulated with niches and richly decorated with coloured marble slabs and mosaic. On the northern wall of the hall opens a semi-circular exedra where

The interior of the Vestibule

the emperor himself sat during receptions. On either side of the exedra were stairways to the ground-floor and thus to the southern gate and exit to the sea. The shape and size of this hall probably points to the high credibility of the new suggestions concerning the purpose of the palace. Perhaps the hall was the throne room.

Ground-floor halls - "Diocletian's cellars"

The ground-floor halls ("cellars") are in fact a complex of sub-structures which had the purpose of providing a suit-

Central hall of the ground-floor of Diocletian's palace (Diocletian's cellars)

able basis for the construction of the imperial apartment on the first floor, and at the same time to level off the southern part of the palace because the ground sloped towards the sea. The significance of these structures is enormous, because from them we can reconstruct the disposition and shape of the chambers of the imperial suite with a great degree of certainty. These halls are also important because different forms of architecture of late antiquity can be studied in detail, and the problems of the articulation and technology of load-bearing constructions can be understood. Likewise, these halls are an encyclopaedia of sorts of different spatial solutions of its time, but also certain prototypes of new architectural ideas which appeared with early Christianity. The sub-structure under the "throne" room can testify to that because it is divided by pylons in three parts in which the semi-circular exedra reminds one of apses of the same shape.

The underground halls are well preserved because they were for the most part filled with rubble and other waste materials, although at first they provided shelter for the inhabitants of Salonae.

The largest hall and parts of the eastern halls were excavated in 1945, and systematic excavations have been going on since 1955. These monumental and exceptionally attractive spaces are open to visitors in their entirety on the west side and for the greatest part on the east side. The ceiling of the halls are strong barrel and cylindrical intersecting vaults. The largest hall, the so-called great ground-floor hall serves as a link between the embankment and the Peristyle.

Art exhibitions are held in these halls, often also theatre and other productions. A medieval olive press was discovered in one of the halls. After conservation it is exhibited in the place where it was found.

The Peristyle

The Peristyle is certainly one of the most notable architectural complexes of the palace, of Split and also of the whole East Adriatic area. It is a relatively large open space on the longitudinal axis of the Palace, framed by columns on three sides. The area of the Peristyle is lowered three steps with reference to the level of the streets. In this way, the northern half of the Palace and the two-floor imperial apartment were brought to the same level. The Peristyle is an area which allows access to the imperial apartment on its south side, and it provides communication with the emperor's mausoleum on its east side. On the west side it gives access to three temples of the palace. On the south side, four slender columns with Corinthian capitals carry a triangular gable above a semi-circular arch. Thus they form the *Protiron,* the monumental entrance to Diocletian's apartment. An enclosed imperial loggia is situated between the central columns of the Protiron. The emperor appeared there on special occasions to receive homage from the inhabitants of the palace and other visitors. The festivities were certainly connected with the cult of the imperial deity, and it seems indisputable that the whole complex of the Peristyle was built for the purpose of the religious ritual in which the emperor appeared to his subjects as a living deity, and they worshipped him probably lying prostrate on the pavement of the Peristyle. A monumental sculpture was erected on top of the Protiron gable, probably four horses. A colonnade of six columns each was set on either side of the Protiron, supporting seven arches with richly decorated garlands. Latticed stone fences supported on the base were set between the columns. A door leading east to the emperor's mausoleum and another leading west towards the temples was set in the third space between the columns, counting from the south. In 16th and 17th century Protiron received two chapels, Our Lady of Conception and Our Lady of the Belt, and the cen-

The Peristyle at night

Split Summer, the production of Verdi's Aida at the Peristyle

Richly decorated capital of the mausoleum of Diocletian

tral arch. Diocletian's temple-mausoleum, situated on the east side of the Peristyle, was converted into the cathedral, for which a tall, monumental belfry was built in 13th and 14th century. At the end of the eastern part of the Peristyle is a small Renaissance church of St. Roc, converted in 1516 from an earlier Romanesque house. Medieval houses were later built in the areas between the columns on the west side.

The Peristyle is an exceptional stage for theatre and music productions of the Split summer festival named "Split Summer". Productions of Verdi's "Aida" can be especially successful and attractive.

Emperor Diocletian's mausoleum - the cathedral of Split

The monumental *Mausoleum of emperor Diocletian* is to the east of the Peristyle. It is situated in a quadrangular yard surrounded by a high wall. It is a temple of a central type with outside passage. It is formed by columns surrounding

an octagonal building, and is covered with faceted stone ceiling. The interior of the temple is of circular plan articulated with semi-circular and quadrangular niches. Two rows of

Bust of Diocletian on the garland under the cupola of the mausoleum

Cupola of Diocletian's mausoleum (today the cathedral)

Bust of Diocletian's wife, Empress Prisca, on the garland under the cupola of the mausoleum

vertical columns of precious coloured stone carry richly decorated bands. The garland beneath the dome is figurative in character. It carries portraits in relief of the emperor Diocletian and his wife, empress Prisca framed with laurel wreaths which are held by winged boys. The same garland has a hunting scene, which is a motif characteristic of the funerary cult and so it indirectly points to the function of the building. The dome was originally covered with mosaic. A porphyry sarcophagus with the body of the emperor stood in the centre of the mausoleum, but it was removed in early Middle Ages. A quadrangular entrance - prostasis - stood originally in front of the temple to the west. A high Romanesque cathedral belfry was built in this place in the Middle Ages. A circular *crypt* is below the mausoleum, which in the Middle Ages was converted to *the church of St. Lucy*.

In the period when the palace became a city, the mausoleum became the *cathedral of St. Mary*. However, very early it was named the *church of St. Domnius,* a martyr from Solin, whose altar was erected in the cathedral in Early Middle

Crypt of Diocletian's mausoleum (later church of St. Lucy)

Ages. At the same time a door was opened on the south side of the cathedral. The area of the cathedral choir was added on the east side of the building in 17th century, during the Baroque period.

The cathedral belfry

The monumental *belfry of St. Domnius* was built in the area of the prostasis, the entrance to the temple, in 13th century and in early 14th century. All architectural elements show Romanesque characteristics, the new Gothic spirit is felt in a certain elongation and elaboration of the system of openings. Another Romanesque level was added in early 14th century, and the belfry was completed in a mixed Gothic-Renaissance style. This harmonious slender and monumental edifice has for long centuries determined the visual identity of the city, particularly when viewed from the sea; so it appeared in the historical coat-of-arms of the city as early as the Middle Ages. As the belfry gradually became dilapidated during its long history, a thorough reconstruction was made at the close of 19th century. Many sections of the original Romanesque sculpture were replaced with new copies, and pieces of the original sculpture are kept in the Split City Museum. In the spirit of the ideas on the purity of style prevalent at the time, the original Gothic-Renaissance level was replaced with a neo-Romanesque one. The reconstruction of the belfry was all too radical, with a builders' precision and coldness characteristic of the 19th century historicism, and the vivacity of the original, which can still be seen on old photographs of Split, was lost in the process.

Two strong Romanesque lions at the entrance to the belfry have been preserved of the original sculptural decoration. They are similar in character to the lions at the portal of the cathedral of Trogir. Scenes from the Annunciation and Christ's Nativity have remained in the original positions on the first floor. The subtlety of execution and elegance is also linked to the workshop of Master Radovan who was working

Approach to the cathedral from the Peristyle

Cathedral belfry viewed through the arches of the Peristyle

in Trogir at the same time in 13th century. Considerably more rough and robust are the relief carvings showing St. Stasius, St. Domnius, and St. Peter, bearing the signature of Master Otho, obviously a sculptor of northern origin from 13th century. The arch with the hunting scenes under the vault of the belfry is attributed to the same master.

The portal of the cathedral

One of the most valuable and best preserved specimens of medieval woodcarving on the east coast of the Adriatic, and for their characteristics also one of the more important monuments of the kind in the world, are the carved wood door panels of the cathedral. They were made in 1214 in the Romanesque style by the painter and woodcarver Andrija Buvina, who worked in Split in the first half of 13th century. His family name suggests that the artist was doubtless of Slavic origin.

The door panels are made of walnut over oak planks. They are 530 cm high and 360 cm wide. They have two leafs. Each leaf has fourteen scenes from Christ's life separated into richly ornamented cassettes. The left leaf shows scenes from Christ's childhood and public activity, from the Annunciation to Lazarus raised to life, and the right leaf shows Christ's Passion, death and Ascension. A mixture of two concepts can be observed in the scenes: one static, with linear styling of Byzantine origin, the other narrative, dynamic, and picturesque, reaching completely the style of contemporary western trends. The area between the cassettes is filled with bands decorated with the motifs of curling vines and bunches of grape, birds pecking at grapes, little figures of grape-gatherers, or figures of fantastic character holding on to leaves of buds.

The whole area of the door panels creates a lively game of light and shadow with the richness of ornament and richness of figural representation. The carved forms are specially emphasised with a specific polychromy. The background was painted red, and all figures in relief were originally gilded.

34

Interior of the cathedral. Romanesque pulpit on the left, baroque altar of St. Domnius in the centre, altar of St. Stasius on the right.

Buvina's door panels are a rare example in his time of such a complex plastic expression realised in wood in the seaboard region, which is characterised by stone ornaments.

Left:

Andrija Buvina, the portal of the cathedral from 1214

Andrija Buvina, scenes from Christ's life - details of the portal

The interior of the cathedral

To The left of the entrance is a monumental, richly decorated *stone pulpit* executed in the late Romanesque style (13th-14th c.). The hexagonal pulpit richly articulated with a row of blind arcades with double columns of multicoloured marble, scenes in relief and symbols of the Evangelists rests upon six slender columns with exceptionally vividly decorated capitals.

Romanesque pulpit of the cathedral, 13th-14th c.

Some twenty years later, in 1448, the maste Juraj Matejev Dalmatinac built the *altar of S Stasius* in the north-eastern niche of the cathe dral, achieving the ultimate in Gothi Renaissance sculpture on our coast. Havin adapted to the concept and form to Bonino's a tar, Juraj Dalmatinac has achieved a unity c form with the disposition of masses, plasticit and exceptional quality of sculpture in balanc with the decorative elements, which testifies t his exceptional talent and artistic skill. Of esp cial quality is the relief representing the scourg ing of Christ.

*Richly decorated Romanesque
capitals of the cathedral pulpit*

Wooden choir stalls, richly decorated in the Romanesque style, were placed into the Baroque choir which was built in 17th century. The stalls were carved in the 13th century and reveal the influence of Lombardian Romanesque style, but also of Byzantine and Islamic decoration. Carvings with animal and plant motifs are arranged in seven horizontal zones with turned gratings and distinct geometrical interlacing. Carved wood reliefs of patron saints of Split are set on the four ends of the back rest.

The altar of St. Domnius is situated in the south-east niche of the cathedral. It consists of an Early Christian sarcophagus with characteristic decorative motif of the strigil and a pre- Romanesque panel with wicker decoration. The sculptor Bonino of Milan executed a new one above it in 1427 in the spirit of Late Gothic. The scene is dominated by the figure of the saint in supine position under a stone canopy, and the antependium shows figures of saints. The stone ciborium by the same master was painted in the spirit of Gothic painting by the local painter Dujam Vušković.

Cathedral, figurative details of the choir seats. Carving from 13th c.

The northern, *Baroque altar of St. Domnius* was built in 1766-67 by the well-known Venetian sculptor and altar builder G. K. Morlaiter. The richly articulated altar consists of a sarcophagus supported by allegorical female figures of Faith and Perseverance/Constancy. The martyrdom of the first Salonitan bishop is shown on the antependium in softly modelled relief.

The high altar of the cathedral is also made in the baroque style and it is located in the choir which was added to the building. The vault above the altar was painted by the native master Matija Pončun in the Baroque period.

The cathedral has several valuable crucifixes from various style periods.

The vestry, which was added on the south-eastern side, contains the *cathedral treasury* with numerous valuable sacral objects of art from Early Middle Ages to the Baroque period. Primarily these are various reliquaries and liturgical objects of precious metals, liturgical books and old manuscripts, icons and valuable mass vestments. The Split Book of Gospels from 7th-8th c. is considered among the most valuable objects. The richly decorated manuscript *Historia Salonitana,* chronicle of the church of Split, written in 13th century by Thomas the Archdeacon, is of particular importance. It is one of the most important medieval historical sources for the study of the history of Split and the whole territory of Dalmatia.

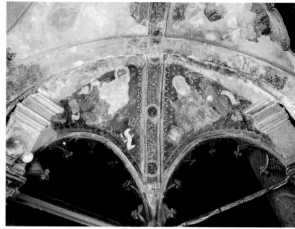

*Frescoes in the ciborium of the altar of St. Domnius.
Painted by Dujam Vušković in 1429*

*Juraj Dalmatinac:
Scene of Christ's scourging, detail from the altar of
St. Stasius, 1448*

*Split cathedral, altar of St. Domnius,
by Bonino of Milan, 1427*

*Split cathedral, the altar of St. Stasius,
by Juraj Dalmatinac, 1448.*

Left:
The northern, baroque altar of St. Domnius,
by G. M. Morlaiter, 1766-1767

Below left:
Scenes from Mary's life, the vault of the baroque
altar of St. Domnius. Attributed to Marco
Capogrosso, 17th c.

Jupiter's temple - the baptistery of the cathedral

On the west side, in the axis of the mausoleum, is the *quadrangular ("Jupiter") temple.* It is of quadrangular plan, with raised floor and six columns which form a porch on the east side. The columns and the porch are not preserved, in contrast to the perfectly preserved cella with cassetted barrel vault. An Egyptian sculpture of the Sphinx is front of the temple. In Christian times the temple was converted in the *baptistery of the cathedral,* and its crypt into a miniature *church of St. Thomas.* The *sarcophagus of Archbishop Ivan* (of Ravenna), the founder of the diocese in the

new town, decorated with the motif of a lily in relief, is in the baptistery, and the *sarcophagus of Archbishop Lawrence* from 11th century, who was at the head of the church of Split at the time of Croatian national rulers. The *baptismal font* was probably built in 12th century. It is in the form of a cross. It is obvious that it was made from panels that once made part of an altar rail, perhaps the rail in the cathedral. The panels are richly ornamented with wicker motifs; among them stands out the panel with the relief of a pentagram and birds pecking at grapes. Of especial historical importance, but also artistically valuable is a stone tablet from 11th century on the front section of the baptismal moulding representing a Croatian ruler on the throne. The style of the relief point to a possible period of execution which brings the effigy of the ruler in a possible connection with King Dmitar Zvonimir. A bronze statue of St. John the Baptist from 1954. is also in the baptistery, a late work of the famous sculptor Ivan Meštrović.

In the Middle Ages (11th century) a belfry was built over the baptistery, consisting of three levels with smaller double windows, but it was demolished in 19th century.

Left:
Baptismal font from the cathedral baptistery in the shape of a cross (Jupiter's temple)

Sudamja - the feast of st. Domnius

St. Domnius, the patron saint of Split, came from Syria. The local tradition from early Middle Ages has it that he was a disciple of St. Peter himself. This account, which originated from Ivan (of Ravenna), the first bishop of Split, was invented for the purpose of establishing the idea that the church of Split had Apostolic origins. It is an undeniable historic fact that he was a Christian teacher and the first bishop of Salonae, who died as a martyr at the close of the 3rd century of

Feast of St. Domnius, procession with the relics of the saint

Feast of St. Domnius, popular costumes in the procession

The feast of St. Domnius, solemn mass in the open in front of the cathedral

the beginning of the 4th during severe persecution under Diocletian. He was buried at Solin. The former Diocletian's mausoleum, which had in the meantime become a Christian church, was soon referred to as the church of St. Domnius. This is in a way an exceptional example of historical justice and fate of the persecutor and the persecuted. From the early Middle Ages St. Domnius (Duje) is considered the principal patron of the city of Split. His feast on May 7, in addition to being a religious feast, is the most important popular feast in Split. Besides most solemn mass rites it also comprises an attractive solemn procession with the relics of the saint through the historical core of Split with the participation of the citizens of Split and their associations.

The buildings on the west side of the Peristyle

Two smaller temples of circular plan with an outer passage surrounded by columns, dedicated to *Cybele* and *Venus,* are preserved only in fragments built into the houses to the west of the Peristyle.

A Romanesque-Early Gothic palace stands in the south-west corner of the Peristyle. It went through several modifications during the Renaissance, and the Baroque period brought a balcony which juts out of the Peristyle façade. Remains of a circular temple of Cybele from the times of most identical in size with the neighbouring temple of Cybele. Although investigations found a circular floor, a description from 16th century states that the temple was hexagonal on the outside. It is possible that a hexagonal cella surrounded with columns was built over a circular base. The Romanesque loggia was part of the old town hall which later came into the possession of the Grisogono family, one of the oldest noble families of Split. The palace was partitioned in 15th century. Its southern part came in the possession of the Cipci family, as witnessed by the coat-of-.arms on its southern portal built in flowery Gothic style and characteristic of the workshop of Juraj Dalmatinac. The Cipci family added another floor in late 16th century. It was built in the Renaissance style, and is probably from the workshop of Nicholas of Florence. Recently renovated, it is one of the best examples of renaissance architecture in Split.

A complex of *western baths* was discovered to the south-west of the baptistery. The remains are similar to those found within the framework of the eastern baths, which suggests the same method of heating and water supply. Because of their proximity to Diocletian's apartment, it is probable that they were at the disposal of the emperor himself.

A view of Grisogono-Cipci palace through the arches of the Peristyle

Pylons from the porch in the antique street within Diocletian's Palace

Diocletian were found within the palace in 1957. They had been integrated into the building. A considerable section of the floor and of the crypt were found as well as segments of columns. Judging by the remains, the temple was cylindrical in shape, with a diameter of 9.5 metres, and was surrounded with columns which thus formed the outside passage. The cella was built over a crypt.

The *Grisogono-Cipci palace* is situated along the north-west part of the Peristyle. It appears to have grown into the western colonnade of the Peristyle. Alterations in the "Luxor" coffeehouse on the ground-floor of the palace has revealed the floor of the temple of Venus and of a Romanesque *loggia* with preserved columns, capitals and arches. The temple of Venus is al-

Baroque Cindro palace in the decumanus, transverse street within Diocletian's palace

house is cut by a transverse medieval street (the present-day Papalićeva ulica) with the large complex of the Late Gothic *Papalić palace*. It is one of the most beautiful Gothic-Renaissance palaces in Split, from the workshop of the master Juraj Dalmatinac. A one-story loggia is in the yard of the palace, and the first floor is reached by an external stairway. A large hall on the first floor has a beautiful monumental quadruple window. The

The court of Papalić palace, today Museum of the City of Split, 15th c.

The monuments in the northern part of the palace

A *classicist palace* of simple, restrained lines and harmonious proportions is situated in the transverse street - decumanus - close to the east gate. In 19th century it served as the building of the Grammar School. The representative *Cindro palace* is situated at the western end of the decumanus, one of the most beautiful examples of secular Baroque architecture in Split.

Of the original *west street* that ran along the west wall of the Palace it is only the arches at the intersection with the with the west gate that have been preserved. In place of the street from classical antiquity there is a narrowed medieval street (Ulica Julija Bajamontija). Few fragments have remained of a large *north-west house*. The *north street,* which ran along the inner side of the northern wall of the palace, was transformed into a medieval street with a lot of preserved architectural elements from the period. The *north-east house* has left only fragments of floor mosaics. Original massive *pylons of a porch* that ran along the walls of the palace have been preserved in the *east street.* The area of the former north-east

City of Split Museum is housed in the building. It has collections of various art objects, fragments of sculpture and stone ornaments which were parts of the historical buildings, historical coats-of-arms, weapons, documents, engravings, maps and old photographs as well as other museum pieces that are important for the history of Split. The arrangement of the museum collections was thoroughly renewed in 1992. The museum is establishing a gallery, *Galerija Vidović,* devoted to the most significant Split painter of 20th century and one of the principal protagonists of modern Croatian painting.

Coat-of-arms of the Papalić family

Exhibition hall in the Split City Museum

45

Narodni trg

Narodni trg (People's square) is situated to the west of the Palace. As early as the Middle Ages it has been the city centre. According to available sources, since 13th century the defence yard of the West Gate of the Palace was a place where public documents were made. This indicates that the administrative centre of Medieval Split gradually shifted towards the new, western part of the city, which grew out of the former western suburb with the building of new city walls in 14th century.

The square formed in the area around the pre-Romanesque *church of St. Lawrence,* and it was long named after it. Later it was named Arms square and Square of the Signiors. It acquired its full function as the municipal centre in the period between 14th and 16th c., when several municipal buildings in the flowery Gothic style were completed. The complex comprised the Rector's palace and the Communal palace with the City Loggia in the east part of the ground-floor. Other public functions, such as the old theatre and the prison were also within the same complex. This was certainly the most important example of secular Gothic architecture in Split. The church of St. Lawrence was probably demolished in order to provide space for it. The new open space originally had the form of a triangle, which was lost due to extension achieved by thoughtless demolition of a great part of the communal palace complex in 1821. Only the Gothic *City Loggia with the city hall* stands today, housing

People's Square at night

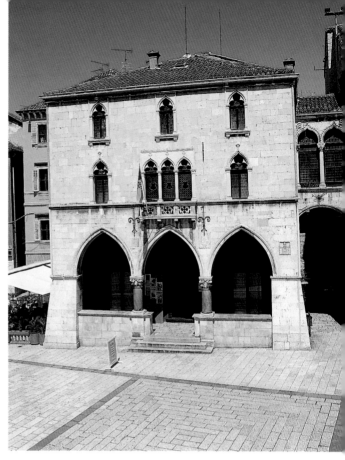

Scene from People's Square

*Communal Palace at Narodni trg, built in 15th c.,
completely renovated in 19th c.*

the Ethnographic museum. The building has kept its original form on the ground-floor only, where three strong Gothic arches in its central part are supported by two columns with capitals, thus limiting the area of the City Loggia. The upper part of the building lost its original form during two radical renovations, in 1826-30 and in 1890. The upper level which had a large Gothic triple window has now two new Neo-Gothic windows. The medieval coat-of-arms of Split from 14th century is built into the southern façade. It shows the façade of the Palace of Diocletian and the cathedral belfry in stylised forms.

The *Ethnographic Museum* was founded in 1910 by purchase of the complete inventory of the large provincial exhibition of folk art and artefacts which was held in Split then. In the course of time the collections were enriched considerably in the course of systematic investigation in the wider area around Split. The museum has precious materials of folk creation from the territory of Dalmatia. It is all the more important because the great social and economic changes that occurred in 20th century have caused almost

complete disappearance of folk art and traditional village crafts. Of particular value are the collections of old, original folk costumes from around Split, from the islands of central Dalmatia, and from the continental hinterland. The collection of folk jewellery is significant and numerous objects from which the inventory of old Dalmatian cottages can be reconstructed, as well as the original folk tools and other objects which testify to the forms of folk life.

The *Karepić palace,* built in 16th century in the style of High Renaissance, leans against the City Hall with which it is connected by a beautiful Late Gothic double window.

An interesting Romanesque *house-fort* with Romanesque openings on the first floor stands on the eastern side of the square, just north of the west gate of the Palace of Diocletian. The city clock with the dial divided into 24 hours was set above it in 15th century. It was partly reconstructed from the parts which were preserved. A small *Gothic bell-house* was built above the fort in 15th century. To the south, opposite the Romanesque fort, is an interesting late-Romanesque *Ciprian de Ciprianis Palace* from 1394. A relief

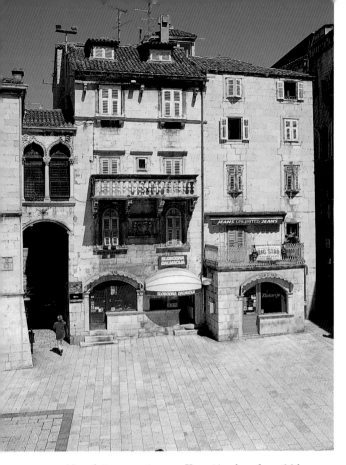

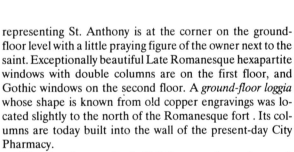

Narodni trg, renaissance Karepić palace from 16th c.

Romanesque house-tower with Gothic belfry and renaissance clock

representing St. Anthony is at the corner on the ground-floor level with a little praying figure of the owner next to the saint. Exceptionally beautiful Late Romanesque hexapartite windows with double columns are on the first floor, and Gothic windows on the second floor. A *ground-floor loggia* whose shape is known from old copper engravings was located slightly to the north of the Romanesque fort . Its columns are today built into the wall of the present-day City Pharmacy.

The Renaissance *Pavlović Palace* stands on the south side of the square. On the ground floor it has architectural elements of an earlier Romanesque building. Of the same Romanesque style are the windows which are noticeable in outline on the present-day Hotel "Central" located next to the Pavlović Palace.

The west side of the square is closed by the monumental *Nakić House,* designed in 1902 as a residential and business building by Špiro Nakić, architect from Split. It was built in the spirit of the contemporary trends of Viennese Secession with rounded corners and rich decoration typical of the style. This building is a rare example of the representative Secession architecture in Dalmatia.

Nakić house at the People's Square built in the style of Vienna Secession

A very old street, nowadays called Bosanska, leads north from the People's Square. During the Middle Ages it served as the principal artery connecting the main square to the north gate - *Vrata od Pisture* - which is preserved close to the north-east corner tower of the Palace. The *Cambi Palace* is at one end of the street, built in the Late Gothic style. It has a marked tripartite window on the first floor.

Marulićeva ulica leads south towards the sea. The large Baroque *Benedetti Palace* takes the greater part of its east side.

Left:
Coat-of-Arms of the city of Split, built into the front of the Communal palace, 14 th century

Domaldova ulica leads to the north from the north-west corner of the square. A Late Gothic palace from 15th century is situated on the east side of the street. It is said to have belonged to the poet *Marko Marulić*. The western side of the street used to be taken by the large block of the Benedictine nunnery of *St. Mary "de Taurello"*, founded in 11th century. Fragment only have been preserved of the convent and the basilica, the Gothic south portal from 14th century, and the atrium from the late phase (18th century). The *Church of the Holy Spirit* is situated at the north end of the street. It contains the tomb of Andrija Alješi, famous sculptor and architect of Albanian origin, at first assistant to Juraj Dalmatinac in the construction of the cathedral of Šibenik, and later an independent architect and sculptor with his own workshop in Split. His most important work is the baptistery of the Trogir cathedral.

Trg braće Radić (Voćni trg)

Trg braće Radić (Voćni trg) is situated to the south of Narodni trg, almost at the sea. It was formed in a filled-in cove. Its south side is closed by the forts of the *citadel*. It was built in 1453 for the Venetian garrison, and its walls were washed by the sea. Similar citadels were built during the early years of Venetian rule in other Dalmatian cities as well, Zadar and Trogir. Their purpose was twofold. Doubtless, they were intended to protect the city from possible danger; but the detached position in which the garrison of the new rulers was isolated from the city speaks of the certain insecurity of the new authorities based on the experience of numerous revolts of citizens, particularly in Zadar. In this sense, the Venetian citadel was at the time of its construction also a threat to the citizens of Split. It was a polygonal building with high defence walls of stone. Only the two monumental towers and the gate between them have remained to the present.

The north side of the square is closed by an imposing baroque *Milesi palace* from 18th century. Excellently positioned so that it does not dominate the square, with its dimensions, harmonious but not too obtrusive architectural elaboration of a three-story façade it still reminds the viewer of the Renaissance order. The ground-floor has five arched openings. It is an important example of the representative residential baroque architecture, in Split as well as in Dalmatia. The Institute of scientific and art work of the Croatian Academy of Arts and Sciences is situated in the palace. A large exhibition hall is on the first floor, the venue of numerous art and other cultural events. In front of the palace, on a high stone pedestal, rises a

Brothers Radić Square, monument to Marko Marulić by Meštrović. Front of Milesi palace in the background

bronze monument of the great Croatian poet *Marko Marulić,* the work of the sculptor Ivan Meštrović.

The west part of the square opens to the west of the Milesi Palace. Formerly it was named Krušni trg or Trg zeleni. Šubićeva ulica runs north from it. The east side of the street has the baroque *Tartaglia Palace,* and the west side the so-called *Little Papalić Palace.* Its ground-floor is from the Romanesque period (13th c.), and the additions are from 14th century. In the 15th century it was modified again by the master Juraj Dalmatinac, who executed the portal and the double windows in flowery Gothic style.

The famous embankment, popular promenade and meeting place of all generations

The embankment

The front of the historical core of the city of Split facing the sea has with the passage of time become an attractive promenade particularly trough land fill and the construction of the embankment in 19th century. For its appearance and because of the surrounding buildings it provides a most impressive view of Split and is certainly the most attractive waterfront promenade among the seaboard cities of the east Adriatic coast.

The present-day Obala hrvatskog narodnog preporoda (Croatian National Revival Embankment) is a straight, wide stretch of a sea promenade. On the land side, for its full length of almost 200 metres, the southern façade of Diocletian's Palace with all the picturesque additions grown into the structure of the ancient Roman architecture opens to the sea. A series of large buildings with numerous coffee-houses, shops and tourist agencies on the ground-floor, from the second half of 19th century, continues towards the west. In the west the promenade ends in a large representative square called Prokurative, built in neo-Renaissance forms, and a well with a fountain in front of it. Along the promenade is a line of tall palms, and the whole area is arranged horticulturally. A view of the city port, the marina, the hill Marjan, the whole gulf of Split and the islands in the offing opens from the promenade. Being a pedestrians' zone, the embankment is the favourite meeting-place of the inhabitants of Split of all generations. Throughout the year it is crowded and teeming with life, which contributes to its picturesqueness and attraction. It is a sort of window of the city and its citizens.

The central building of the Prokurative, mid 19th c.

Marmontova ulica and Prokurative

The western limit of the old city core is the street with the name of Napoleon's marshal Marmont, the man who during his short rule performed important undertakings of renovation and modernisation of Split. Many roads were built, the embankment and the city lighting regulated, the western ramparts removed and a park planted in their place, and undisturbed westward spreading of the city facilitated. The street descends to the promenade at right angles. Although in the past it was one of the principal thoroughfares, it is now a promenade.

A large architectural complex of the *Prokurative,* obviously named after the famous Venetian original, is situated on the west side of the street. It was built on the insistence of the mayor Bajamonti at the place of a former park planted by the French marshal Marmont. The complex consists of three architectural wholes - the north building whose front is facing the sea, and the east and west wings enclosing a square which is opened to the sea promenade over a flight of steps. The buildings were designed in the neo-Renaissance style, with arcaded porches in the wings, and have exerted markedly influence on the definition of the western part of the city near the shore. The building was relatively slow. The oldest, north wing where the old theatre (Bajamonti theatre) was situated, was completed in 1859. The west wing was built in 1864-1865. The east wing took a long time, and was completed in 1929. A *monumental fountain* (named Bajamontuša) was built in front of the Prokurative to celebrate the reconstruction of the waterworks in 1880. It was demol-

The northern part of the historic core

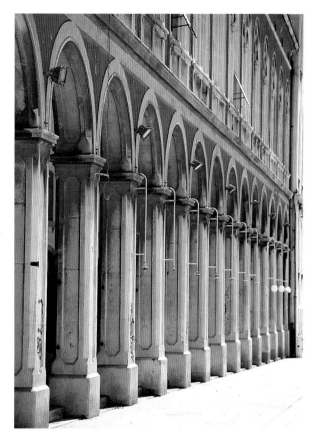

Arcades of the porch at Prokurative (around 1865)

On leaving the historic core by way of Bosanska ulica and the north gate, Vrata od Pisture, on the east side we can observe the remains of a large medieval *Benedictine nunnery*. It spread along a considerable part of the north face of Diocletian's Palace. It was founded in 1069, and for long centuries it enjoyed great reputation and it acquired much real property. In 1807, during Napoleon's administration, all monasteries and convents were dissolved, and the Benedictine nuns left Split. The abandoned buildings were in the thirties converted to a military hospital by the Austrian authorities. The church and the convent suffered heavily in a conflagration in 1878. The remains of the buildings along the north face of the palace were cleaned after World War II, and parts of three buildings were preserved. One is the pre-Romanesque *church of St. Benedict (St. Euphemia),* built even before the foundation of the convent, around the middle of 11th century. Only the lower parts of its walls are

ished in 1948, and a well with a fountain was built in its place. The area ion from of the Prokurative is used nowadays for music and other events in the open. The traditional Split festival of light music is best known among them. The monumental *Bajamonti palace* (later Dešković Palace) with harmonious neo-Renaissance front was built to the west of the fountain. Remains of the pentagonal defence rampart, the so-called *Baščun* which was part of the fortifications in 17th century, can be seen at the northern end of the street.

The building of the *Sulphur baths*, designed in 1903 by the architect Kamilo Tončić of Split, stands out on the east side of the street. It was built in the spirit of Viennese Secession with an abundance of singular architectural decoration on the front.

Secession ornament on the building of the Sulphur baths (architect K. Tončić, 1903)

Remains of the early medieval church of St. Benedict (St. Euphemia) at the northern wall of the Palace of Diocletian

preserved and presented today. It was a three-nave basilica with inscribed transept and three semi-circular apses. The *chapel of the blessed Arnir,* built as an addition to the church in the style of Early renaissance, the work of the master Juraj Dalmatinac in 1444, is also preserved. Arnir was archbishop of Split who was murdered in 1180 by the inhabitants of Poljica in the Mosor mountain during the determination of estate boundaries. The altar of the blessed Arnir, also the work of Juraj, is represented by a plaster cast in

Chapel of the Blessed Arnir, 15th c.

Following page:
Ivan Meštrović, Monument to bishop
Gregory of Nin, 1929

The belfry of the blessed Arnir from 18th c. was situated within the complex of the former Benedictine abbey

out, the whole complex together with the bastion was adapted as a museum, but its purpose is not defined yet. The Cornaro bastion is a typical baroque polygonal fort, and is the best preserved of all similar fortifications in Split, although its top was cut off in 1934 for the purpose of regulating the traffic. The *City Park* was planted in 1860 in the place of an earlier wall which linked two polygonal bastions.

the *Dominican monastery* was founded in 1217 along the east wall of the palace. The existing church was enlarged at the close of the last century, and widened in 1932, so only parts of the former baroque building are preserved in the central nave.

The city spread radially after the demolition of fortifications, and new suburbs grew around it: *Lučac* in the east, *Manuš* and *Dobri* in the north, and *Veli Varoš* in the west. The independent *Gripe tower* was erected in 17th century to the north-east of Lučac. Military barracks was built there around the middle of 19th century. The building was adapted as the *Croatian Maritime Museum.*

Fountain in the centre of the City park, around 1860

the chapel, and the original is in the parish church of Kaštel Lukšić. The upper part shows the body of the blessed Arnir on a bier with an expressive scene of mourning. The scene of the martyrdom is shown on the antependium in low relief. The slender, tall *belfry of the blessed Arnir* was formerly also part of the Benedictine complex. It was built in 18th century. A monumental bronze *statue of Gregory of Nin*, the work of Ivan Meštrović from 1929, stands to the east of the belfry, opposite the north gate of the Palace. It was planned for the Peristyle, where it had stood originally. However, it did not fit there because of its mass; so it was moved to its present position in 1954.

The complex of the *old City Hospital,* built on the *Cornaro bastion,* is situated to the north of these monuments. The hospital was begun in 1872. The building is constructed in a classicist style. When the hospital was moved

Front of the Croatian national Theatre of Split (1893)

Trg Gaje Bulata

The *Croatian National theatre* is situated on Gajo Bulat Square in the suburb of Dobri. it was built between 1891 and 1893 in the neo-Renaissance style to the designs of the architects Vecchietti and Bezić. As the Bajamonti theatre was destroyed in a fire, the new theatre was planned as an independent building, as was the case with all new theatre buildings of the time. Because of the space required for such a structure, it was built outside the historic core of the city. For its size and furnishings it was among the largest and most attractive theatres in all Croatian lands. The face of the building looking towards the square has the marks of a neo-Renaissance style with exceptionally rich decoration on the second floor at the base of the central semi-circular glazed openings. The architectural fragmentation and decoration

of the sides is considerably more subdued. The interior has three rows of boxes and a gallery. The building was heavily damaged in a great fire of 1971. It was thoroughly repaired in 1979.

The front, the atrium, and the foyer were preserved completely, while every effort was made in the restoration of the auditorium to restore the stylistic features of the original building. The west part containing the stage and accessory areas was built anew. The theatre has a full drama and opera ensembles with the ballet troupe, and for its art achievements it is one of the most important theatres in Croatia. This institution is responsible for the organisation of the summer festival - "Splitsko ljeto" - and the drama festival "Marulićevi dani".

Church of Our Lady of Health, built in 1936 from the designs of L. Horvat

Church of Our Lady of Health, Christ King, fresco by I. Dulčić from 1959

The *Church and Monastery of Our lady of Health* is situated on the same square, to the north of the theatre. The monastery is from 17th century, and only the belfry is original. A new church was built in 1936 to the designs of architect Lavoslav Horvat in place of the old church which was pulled down. It is a beautiful example of modern sacral architecture from the period between the two great wars. The famous Croatian painter Ivo Dulčić painted in 1959 a colos-

sal, artistically impressive fresco of Christ the King (9.6 by 19.5 m). A new monastery edifice was built in 1985 after the designs of the architect S. Rožić to the east of the church.

Veli Varoš

The largest and most interesting suburb is the western suburb of Veli Varoš, situated at the eastern slopes of the hill Marjan. It abounds in specimens of folk architecture which are excellently preserved and in original folk settings. In addition, it contains important architectural monuments. The most interesting is the pre-Romanesque *Church of St. Mikula*, built in 11th century. It has kept its original view with a rectangular apse and inscribed transept with a cupola above it. The portal on the western façade, built in the Romanesque style, is decorated with figures of lionesses. The original cupola was probably replaced with a low belfry. The portal bears the inscription recording a citizen named Ivan and his wife Tiha. In the interior, four monolith columns with pre-Romanesque capitals carry the construction of two cylindrical intersecting vaults. The parish *Church of the Holy Cross* was built in 1681, but it was thoroughly modified around the middle of 19th century. The belfry with the bulb-shaped cupola is the only element of the original architecture that has been preserved. The *monastery* of the Conventual Franciscans and the *church of St. Francis* are in the south part of Veli Varoš, almost at the waterfront. After their arrival in Split, the Franciscans built a large church in the Late Romanesque style in the place of a smaller church of St. Felix from 11th century. The side walls of the church have Romanesque architectural elements even today. All the four wings of the cloister, built in a transitory Romanesque-Gothic style, are completely preserved. The tombs of numerous personalities of Split are in the church - the chronicler of the church of Split, Archdeacon Thomas (1200 - 1268),

Following page: Medieval church of St. Nicholas at Veli Varoš (11th c.)

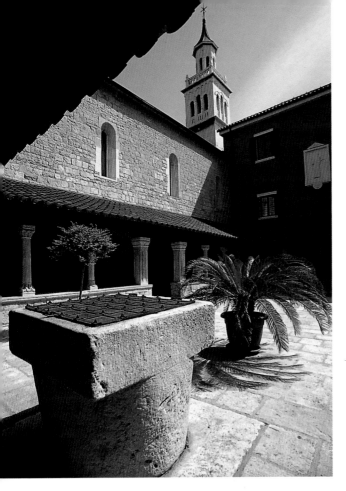

Classicist gloriette at Sustipan

the writer and poet Marko Marulić (1450 - 1524), the composer Ivan Lukačić (1587 - 1649), the poet Jerolim Kavanjin (1643 - 1714), and the politician Ante Trumbić (1864 - 1938) whose sarcophagus, the work of Ivan Meštrović, is placed in the cloister.

Sustipan

The road along the sea under the Marjan hill brings us to the south-east point of the port of Split called *Sustipan* after the former *Monastery of St. Stephen "under the pines"*. The monastery was built in Early Middle Ages. It lost its importance with time; son in early 19th century a small church was built in lace of the older 13th century basilica.

The first cemetery outside the bounds of the city was organised at Sustipan in early 19th century. A classicist gloriette, preserved to the present day, gave the cemetery its special tone. The cemetery was moved to the Lovrijenac area in 1958 - 1962, and a promenade was established at Sustipan. The remains of the medieval basilica and monastery were excavated and conserved on the same occasion.

Sustipan is nowadays an exceptionally attractive promenade under tall pine trees admitting a magnificent view of the sea and the islands before Split.

Left: Sarcophagus with lying effigy of dr. Ante Trumbić in the Franciscan monastery

Museum of Croatian Archaeological Monuments

Museum of Croatian Archeological Monuments

The *Museum of Croatian Archaeological monuments* is located in the area of Meje under the south slopes of Marjan. It is one of the capital objects of Croatian culture. It was built in 1975 after the designs of the architect Mladen Kauzlarić. It consists of the administration and the museum buildings. It was founded at the close of the past century in Knin, and from 1947 it is located in Split. The eminent Croatian archaeologist, the late academician Stjepan Gunjača, and manager for many years, has great merits for its preservation, its present location and organisation. This museum is one of the most significant early medieval collections in Europe. Many exceptional stone monuments from the period of Croatian national rulers, representative examples of stone sculpture, and equally significant epigraphic finds from the same period constitute a particular value of the museum. In the great hall of the museum are exposed the reconstructed ciboria from old Croatian pre-Romanesque churches, specimens of church stone furniture, the famous baptismal font of prince Višeslav (around 800), stone fragments with names of Croatian princes such as the inscription of prince Branimir and a panel bearing the name of King Držislav. Of especial value is the sarcophagus of queen Jelena found at Solin. Don Frane Bulić, notable archaeologist, was able to read its inscription after fitting together its numerous fragments. The text on this monument is of great importance for the dating of historical facts from the period of

63

Interior of the Museum of Croatian Archaeological Monuments. Central area with ciboriums from mediaeval churches from the period of the national dynasty.

Porch of the Meštrović Gallery

Galerija Meštrović

the national rulers. Among the stone sculptural fragments of especial interest is the figure of a Croatian dignitary found at Biskupija near Knin and the figure of Our Lady on the gable from the same locality. The collection from the period of the Great Migration, found in Early Croatian necropolises, is very rich and significant. Weapons and spurs from the period of Charlemagne and an exceptional collection of jewellery from the same period are of particular significance. The museum owns a large and important collection of coins. Standing tomb-stones are exhibited in the garden.

Meštrović Gallery is situated in immediate vicinity. It consists of the complex of the residence of the famous sculptor which was built from 1931 and 1939. Ivan Meštrović is the most outstanding Croatian artist of 20th century. Born in the mountainous region of Dalmatia, educated in Split, as early as a student in Vienna he distinguished himself with his exceptional talent and joined the most modern art trends of the time (Secession). Later, in Paris, he was a student and friend of the great Rodin, and achieved international success in Paris, Rome, London. On the basis of the art of Secession, he

Following page:
Meštrović Gallery

Left:
Ivan Meštrović:
Portrait of Olga Meštrović, Split, Meštrović Gallery

had elaborated his own "heroic" style in which he intended to express great political ideas of his time. After World War I, he was more contemplative in his ideas, and inclined toward stylisation Between the two wars he executed a large number of public monuments in our country, but also in the US. After World War II, he settled permanently in the US, where he died in 1962. With his deed of gift to the Croatian people of 1952, his house and a rich collection of his works of art became a public museum collection. His villa was inspired by classical architecture and consists of two symmetrical wings connected with a porch with tall Ionic columns. Many of his distinctive bronze sculptures are exhibited in the open in the garden. The original settings of his villa are partly preserved in the interior, and a large number of his best known statues in marble, wood and bronze are exhibited in the halls. Numerous plaster originals are also stored in the gallery. The gallery is one of the most attractive and most popular museum institutions in Split.

I. Meštrović sculptures in the exhibition halls of Meštrović Gallery

66

Interior of the church of the Holy Cross at Kaštelet with sculptures by Ivan Meštrović

Ivan Meštrović, Removal from the Cross, detail.
Kaštelet, wood relief in the church of the Holy Cross

Kaštelet

In immediate vicinity of the "Meštrović" gallery is *Kaštelet,* formerly belonging to the Capogrosso-Kavanjin family. It came in the possession of Ivan Meštrović in 1939, who adapted it to house a collection of his works. For this purpose he designed the Church of the Holy Cross. He arranged his famous wooden reliefs of scenes from Jesus' life along the side walls, and in the apse he set one of his most mature and best creations - a large wooden statue of crucified Christ which was carved during World war I, inspired by the horrible war affliction and suffering of the people. This work was executed in the spirit of Gothicised expressionism and is contemporary with similar or identical trends in European sculpture. An expressive stone statue of St. john, the author of the Revelation, is situated in the atrium.

Ascent to Marjan opens a wide view of Split and its port

Park-forest Marjan

The *Marjan* peninsula with the hill of the same name is covered with a artificial park-forest, and is a favourite promenade and resort of the citizens of Split. Marjan can be climbed from Veli Varoš over a system of carefully planned flights of steps, landings, and observation points. Soon after the start we come across a very old church of St. *Manda*. From the first observation point, facing east towards the port, one has an exceptional view of the whole city of Split. Above the observation post is the old *Jewish cemetery*, and ascending further towards the west we come to the 13th century *church of St. Nicholas "de seranda"*. The church has Romanesque characteristics and has a small bell-post..

The whole area of Marjan abounds in little churches, some of which are very old. The *Church of Our lady of seven*

Sorrows from 15th century in on the south side, and on a cliff at the extreme point of Marjan is the little pre-Romanesque *Church of St. George* from 9th century. The upper roads which climbs towards the east and the top of Marjan we come across the little *Church of St. Jerome* from the second half of 15th century with the relief of St. Jerome, the work of the sculptor Andrija Alješi. Above it is the *Hermit's cave* from the Middle ages, reconstructed in 16th century. Further to the east along the same road is the little *Betlem church*, originally built in 14th century, but later reconstructed. At the foot of Marjan on the north side we shall find the very old Church of Our Lady of Spinut, which was built in the early Christian period, but its present state exhibits its Romanesque reconstruction. In the 16th century, dur-

Left:
Forested Marjan peninsula. Oceanographic Institute in the foreground

Church of St. Nicholas "de Seranda" on Marjan Hill, 13th c.

ing the renaissance, a small bell-post was built over the western front. Historical documents record other localities with other churches which became dilapidated and disappeared completely.

Natural History Museum with a zoo, founded in 1924, is situated on the road to the top of Marjan. The top is to the west of the museum. Unforgettable view of the whole Split peninsula, of the Central Dalmatian islands, and of the whole Gulf of Kaštela opens from the observation post. At the extreme west point of Marjan in the *Oceanographic institute,* built in 1933 from the designs of the architect Fabijan Kaliterna. The institute is the supreme institution of sea research in Croatia.

Church Betlem on Marjan Hill

Motif from Marjan Hill

Franciscan monastery at Poljud

Poljud

Lorenzo Lotto: Portrait of the bishop Toma Nigris, 16th c.

The are to the north of the Marjan peninsula was formerly a swamp, hence the place-name (Ital. palude - swamp). The church of St. Mary was built in this inhospitable place in Early Middle Ages in the place of a Roman building. The Franciscan friars founded their monastery in the same place in 15th century. The cloister has been preserved to the present day, together with the Renaissance pylons supporting the porch. A tall quadrangular tower with the upper floor jutting out was built on the west side of the cloister. Obviously, when the monastery was founded the area was not safe and the times were not quiet. The church is of simple plan with a quadrangular apse. It has an altar with

Left:
Sport complex at Poljud. Above: football stadium of the Club "Hajduk" (designed by B. Magaš), below:
complex of swimming pools (designed by I. Antić)

a very valuable polyptych by the Venetian painter Girolamo da Santacroce from the middle of 16th century. The polyptych is particularly significant for the history of Split because it shows St. Domnius, the patron of Split, holding the model of the city in his hand. As it is executed with minute details, it is of prime importance for the study of the urban history of the town and its 16th century outlook. The Franciscan monastery at Poljud has a notable collection of art objects, among which the portrait of the bishop Toma Nigris is particularly outstanding. It was executed by a notable Venetian High renaissance painter Lorenzo Lotto.

On the occasion of the Mediterranean Games which were held in Split in 1979, one of the most beautiful *sports complexes* in Croatia was built in close proximity to the monastery. It consists of a great *football stadium* and a system of indoor and outdoor *swimming pools.* Both complexes are first-class architectural creations. The slender and elegant stadium (today managed by the "Hajduk" football club) in the form of a shell with roofed-over auditorium is work of the well-known Croatian architect Boris Magaš, while the indoor swimming pool with self-supporting roof in the shape of a wave was built from the designs of I. Antić.

The *Church of the Holy Trinity,* one of the most significant architectural monuments of Split is situated to the east of the sports complex and Zrinsko-frankopanska ulica, which runs close by its edge. The church was built in 8th or 9th century, and is the best preserved example of a six-conch church building from the Early Middle Ages. Six semicircular apses are arranged around the cylindrical body. The walls are original, but the cupola was renovated on the occasion of protective work in 1972.

Archaelogical Museum

Returning along the Zrinsko-frankopanska ulica from Poljud to the centre of the city, we come the *Archaeological Museum* on its west side. The archaeological museum of Split is the oldest museum institution in this part of Europe. It was founded as early as 1820 at the initiative of the Austrian emperor Francis I, who had visited the newly annexed Kingdom of Dalmatia in 1818. The emperor was enthusiastic with the immense quantities of materials from antiquity that could be seen in Split in the area of Diocletian's Palace, but also in the surroundings of Split, especially at Solin. As that was the time of the domination of classicist taste and aesthetics, the emperor initiated he foundation in Split of an institution to protect and study the remains from classical antiquity. The first museum was built in 1821. It was a small elongated house of classicist character-

Central building of the Archaeological Museum of Split

istics which was built along the east wall of the Palace. Systematic exploration in the vicinity of Split, particularly the excavations of the classical Salonae in the wider area of Solin, as well as of other numerous classical, Early Christian and Early medieval localities in the wider surroundings of the city had produced so large a number of new finds that it was imperative to build a new, considerably larger and more modern museum. The new museum building and the covered porch for the collection of stone fragments were completed just before World War I, in 1912-1914, from the designs of the Vienna architects Ohmann and Kirchstein, but it was definitely furnished and ready for work in 1920, on the occasion of its centenary. Great credit should be given to don Frane Bulić, director of the museum for many years, not only for the historical finds and significant advance of the ar-

chaeological science but also for the furnishing of the new building. The archaeological museum owns today an enormous collection of artefacts, many of which are world-renowned. Of particular value are numerous sarcophagi with figurative designs exhibiting sculptural work of high quality in the spirit of the Hellenistic tradition. Among early Christian finds of great distinction are the sarcophagi with the figure of the Good Shepherd, and especially interesting is a relief from 4th century showing Jews crossing the Red Sea. The collection of stone fragments contains numerous monuments with important inscriptions as well as several preserved and reconstructed mosaics from Solin. The museum has a large collection of sculpture, glass, jewellery and coins from classical antiquity. The museum library, exceptionally rich, is of especial importance for research work.

Art Gallery

The *Art Gallery* of Split is located closer to the city centre, at Lovretska ulica 11, in the district of Lovret. it was founded in 1931, and it was the first Croatian institution of its kind outside Zagreb. Although cramped and in inadequate premises., it is one of the most important institutions for the study of Croatian art of 19th and 20th centuries, but also of earlier periods. It has very rich collections of high quality, and for value and importance is follows closely the national gallery institutions in Zagreb. The gallery has valuable Gothic paintings from 14th and 15th centuries, a relief by the sculptor Andrija Alješi, paintings by the mannerist painter Andrija Medulić from 16th century, and baroque canvas paintings by Frederik Benković from 17th century. It has the richest collection of Dalmatian artists of 19th century. Especially eminent are the works by Croatian artists of the Modern period, from the nineties of the last century to World War I - the painters Vlaho Bukovac, Celestin Medović and Emanuel Vidović, and the sculptors Ivan Rendić, Ivan Meštrović and Branimir Dešković. Of the inter-war trends, outstanding in quality are the works by the painter Marino Tartaglia, Emanuel Vidović, Juraj Plančić, Ignjat Job, Vjekoslav Parać, and others. The gallery has also a representative collection of the works of contemporary Croatian painters, sculptors, and graphic artists.

Archaeological Museum,
Early Christian sarcophagus with the figure of the Good Shepherd

Archaeological Museum, sarcophagus of Hippolytus and Phaedra

Left: Archaeological Museum, Roman mosaic from Salonae

Contents